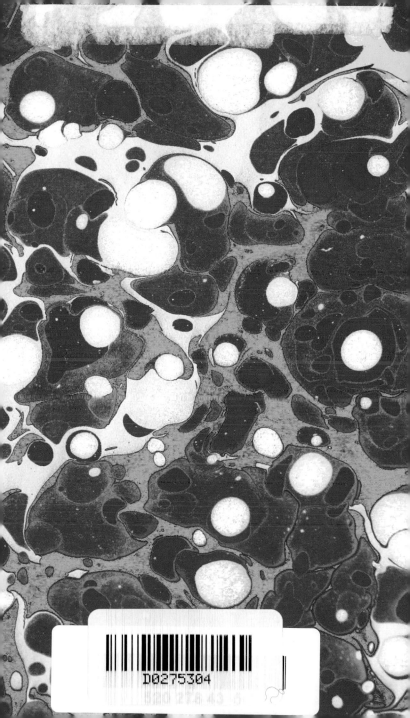

THE DATING GAME

LUCY WATSON

WITH RUTH KELLY

IN LOVE WE TRUST

Quadrille
PUBLISHING

How to activate **SnapTag®**

1 Download the free SnapTag app available at the Google Play Market or iPhone App Store when you search 'SnapTag Reader'.

2 Scan the SnapTag 'LW' logo with your camera. You'll find a logo at the beginning of each chapter.

3 Enjoy the exclusive content. Happy Snapping!

To learn more about SnapTags visit www.spyderlynk.com

CONTENTS

WELCOME TO *THE DATING GAME*, PEOPLE. Way too often, girls fall for players who they know are going to screw them over, or they throw themselves at guys and wonder why they've never heard from them again, or they stay in dead-end relationships because they are too scared of being alone. These girls aren't strangers, they're *me*, they're *my friends*, they're *all of us*. But it's not our fault. Dating nowadays is seriously complicated and the more attached we get to someone the more confusing it seems to become.

That's why I decided to write this book. It's taken a lot of long and painful lessons for me to work out how to play the dating game and I've often wished someone could have just told me the rules from the start, before I had to learn them the hard way.

Don't get me wrong, I'm not saying that I've mastered them all or that I've got a perfect track record. In fact, as you will find out in this book, my experience of cheats, double betrayals and public scandals makes my record far from ideal! But the dating mistakes I've made and the experiences I've had to go through have taught me that I won't put up with anybody who doesn't treat me the way I deserve, ever again. I am never going to settle for just any guy that comes along… it's got to be the right guy. And, hopefully after reading my book, neither will you.

It's about time that we learned how to play men at their own game. In *The Dating Game*, I've hopefully covered all the bases, from being single, to going on first dates and figuring out if he's that interested, to making a relationship work and even how to get over an ex. I want to make sure that if we play the dating game properly none of us will be played *ever* again.

And you know what, our lives are way too short for constant dating dramas! We've all been there; obsessing over unreturned texts or emails; the drunken decision to make that late-night phone call where you say things you *really* don't mean; the bust-ups that end with one of you storming off, hoping the other will follow; those unbelievably awkward it's-not-you-it's-me conversations. I mean, seriously! None of us have enough time or stamina to put up with that level of drama constantly. And we really don't have to put up with them in every relationship. Dating shouldn't be a struggle or packed full of issues that we have to deal with all the time. It should be fun; we only get to do it for a while, so why not enjoy it to the full. What we should do instead, is just try guys on for size and work out if they fit us and not the other way round. This way we won't get too attached, until we know that they are definitely worth our time. And if they don't cut it. It's simple. We need to move on. Next!

One last thing, as you may have already noticed, there are 'LW' SnapTag logos throughout the book. They will be at the start of every chapter. Once you've downloaded the app, you just have to open your SnapTag reader and scan the logo, *et voilà*, a video of me will appear on your phone. In each video, I will give you bits of advice about the next stage of the dating game. So, if you ever need to re-read the first date chapter ahead of an oh-my-god-I'm-nervous date or if you have to jump forward to the break-up stage chapter because your relationship is suddenly over, re-watch my videos in your moments of panic and know that you're not alone. Remember, it's not always easy but not sticking to the dating game and ending up miserable is waaay worse!

Whether you're single, in a relationship or recently broken hearted, now is the time to learn the dating game. I'll be here, along the way, just in case you need me.

1

SINGLE STATUS

IT ALL BEGINS WITH BEING SINGLE
and working out exactly what you want.
We are modern girls who aren't chasing men
or desperate for a guy to define who we are.
We get out of life what we want, when we want.

It used to be embarrassing to admit that you were single. Now, if you say 'I'm single', it means you're pretty hot and you've decided not to settle for some average guy. Instead, you are taking your time to work out what you want out life and who you want to spend it with.

It's kind of obvious, but the best relationship you need to have right now is with yourself. The likelihood is that you will probably spend most of your life with someone else, so working out now what makes you happy is not only really important, but it's also the start of the dating game.

In my life, every day is a 'me' day when I'm single. Not having a boyfriend means that I have more time for my friends, my family, my work and myself. My life just seems to get a little bit overcrowded with a boyfriend. I actually find myself wondering if a guy could fit into my life!

If you have just broken up with your boyfriend, being single can be really hard at first. But trust me, you are better off being single than with someone who makes you feel rubbish. It's this simple: why be miserable with someone when you can be happy alone? Life is way too short to be stuck with some mediocre guy who isn't right for you. I promise you, being single gets better every day and you will eventually reach a stage where you are so happy that it's going to take someone seriously special to make you give up your freedom.

Obviously, although being single is great, there is one thing missing. Nature didn't intend for us to be alone – I do want to share my life with someone. But at the same time, just because I know that would be great, I'm not going to settle for anyone. It's not going to be just any guy, it's going to be the right guy.

Remember, men can make you feel very high and can also make you feel very low, it's all a bit of a risk, but it's all part of the dating game.

SINGLE RULES

Be the best version of you.
Make the most out of what you've got. Go to the gym, get your hair done or buy something you feel seriously hot in. Confidence is best found when single.

Get an early night.
There's a reason why it's called beauty sleep and being tired is never a good look. Get into bed without anything or anybody keeping you awake. When you have a boyfriend, you either stay up late with them or you wait to hear from them.

Enjoy your bed.
One of the best things about being single is that you don't have to share your bed. You get it all to yourself. Although there is lack of regular sex, at least you don't get pestered for it at all hours of the night, because that can be seriously annoying.

Relax.
Do something indulgent and pamper yourself, take a long bath or just watch whatever TV series or film you want. Unwind, life is stress-full. Have some me time.

Do what you want.
You never have to worry about someone else, you can just do what you want, whenever you want. You don't have to set aside a time during the week for your boyfriend. Without realising it, a boyfriend can hold you back as you have to factor them in when you're making plans.

Keep yourself busy.
Make plans and lists of things you want to do.

Spend time with your friends.
Enjoy hanging out together. Go to a restaurant or have a wine-filled evening knowing you have no other commitments. It doesn't have to be a massive night out, as a low-key night in together is just as fun.

Focus on your ambitions.
With no boyfriend issues to distract you, you can focus all your attention and energy on your goals. Whether they're your grades, career or just working out what you want out of life. Personal success is by far the best feeling.

Try to do something you've never done before.
There's so much to do and we are all prone to sticking to our routines. Break out of your 'everyday' comfort-zone and try to do something new every month.

....

Work out what you actually want.
With a completely clear head, work out if you
want a serious relationship right now, a casual
fling or some man-free time.

Responsibility.
What responsibility? You don't have any
commitments to anyone. Enjoy casually flirting;
text whoever you want, meet up with whatever
guy you want and enjoy male attention without
any guilt.

Never **feel sorry for yourself.**
Enjoy being single while it lasts. I guarantee,
when you meet a guy you'll wish back to the
days when you had no commitments.

★ The 5 Rules ★

1. Do whatever you want, whenever
   you want
2. Be the best version of you
3. Go out with your friends
4. Try to do something you've never
   done before
5. Focus on your ambitions

2
LET THE DATING
BEGIN

THE ULTIMATE DATING GAME RULE is that you should date as many guys as you want. Why not? Guys do it all the time. How else are you going to work out what kind of man you want to be with if you don't date different guys. There is literally no point in being exclusive till you know what you really want.

If you are dating someone, but not exclusive yet, it doesn't matter who else you're dating, as you are completely within your single rights to date whoever you want. But don't sleep with them, you don't want to get a reputation and you don't want to get too involved.

If you do develop chemistry with one guy and want to be exclusive, then drop the others, and move forwards with him. Become exclusive. It's that simple. I can always tell when I like one guy more than anyone else, because he becomes the focus of my attention, while the others just start to fade into the background.

After I broke up with H, my first boyfriend of five years, I dated three or four guys at the same time. I didn't sleep with any of them, until I had decided which one I liked the most and we had become exclusive. We went out for a bit but then

I finished it, because the chemistry wasn't there and I wanted to be single again.

The dating game rules mean that you can try guys on for size and see if they fit you and not the other way round.

Meeting guys

The best way to meet a guy is obviously through a friend, but that isn't the only way. You need to be proactive and just get yourself out there. Dating is a numbers game, the more guys you meet the more likely you are to find someone you like. At this stage of the dating game, having mastered being single, you should be feeling pretty confident. If you feel ready, start dating.

Go to dinner parties or organise one with friends. It's a really good way of meeting guys and getting to know them in a relaxed environment. You can chat to guys without the pressure of it being one-on-one and you can see how well they interact with your friends. If you want to host a dinner party, just ask each of your friends to invite a single guy.

Go to bars not clubs to meet a guy.
Guys in clubs can't hear you, so why would they be interested in your personality? All they care about is what you are wearing, and what you'll

look like, with your clothes on their bedroom floor. Bars are much better because they are not too noisy but they're still dark, so you can keep that mysterious vibe going on.

Facebook, Twitter or Instagram.
Not only can you find that guy you met at a party, at work or through a friend, but you can also start casually flirting with them. If they don't add you as a friend, you can still find out a lot about them from their Facebook, Twitter and Instagram pages. However, they can also see you, so don't expect anything serious to come out of it, if you're provocatively dressed in your profile picture. You're selling yourself way too short.

I have to admit, I once messaged a TV actor on Facebook, saying I thought he was really cute (I know). We ended up going on a few dates, but I quickly realised he was just after sex, so I ended it. Looking back, wearing a seriously skimpy outfit in my profile picture could have had something to do with the fact that he only wanted one thing. Realistically, you get back what you put out there. Be safe.

If you do start talking on Facebook; don't message a guy 24:7, keep contact to a minimum. If he really wants to speak to you, he can do it in person. Instant messaging equals zero chemistry. Dating should happen in reality.

Tinder.

Tinder is a genius way to meet someone because by the time you get to speak to them, you already know that they are attracted to you. If they don't interest you – it's just swipe – next!

I used it after I broke up with my ex S – just to see what all the fuss was about, and, yes, to give myself a much-needed ego boost. I arranged to meet up with about five guys, but cancelled last minute because I got seriously cold feet. But quite a few of my friends have met some great guys through Tinder.

Instagram or Snapchat.

If I haven't had any guy attention for a while, I'll take a selfie and add lots of Instagram filters. It works every time – guys always come out of the woodwork. It's kind of embarrassing, but I have got pretty good at taking the perfect selfie:

1. Look in the mirror and play around with finding your best angle.
2. Work out what your best feature is and make the most of it. I like my right-hand profile, so I'll turn my head to the left and tilt it slightly.
3. Scroll through and add the best Instagram filters.
4. Upload. *Et voila.*

Lucy

THE FIRST MOVE

Always let a guy make the first move.
Have fun luring guys over when you're out. The
trick is to make brief eye contact and then look
away (but don't stare or you'll look like a psycho).
This will let him know that you're interested and
if he likes the look of you he will come over. But
never approach a man, men need to approach
you. Men who are interested, will. Men who
aren't, won't. Don't force it. I am all for female
empowerment, but biologically men need to chase
women. It's part of their chemical make-up. Don't
make it too easy, remember you are worth fighting
over the crowds for.

Is he interested and interesting?
This is the best mantra to have in your mind
when you first meet a guy. If he's interesting;
you have common interests and you're attracted
to him. If he's interested; he isn't self-absorbed
and is probably interested and attracted to
you. Simple.

Find out the need-to-know information.
Age, job, relationship status, where they live.
This seems obvious, but if he's leaving something
out there's usually a reason behind it.

DON'T EVER DATE THEM IF...

...They have a girlfriend (or worse are married).
This is the cardinal rule, when it comes to screening guys. Girls should stick together, not screw each other over. I've had other girls make a move on my boyfriend, and it hurts like hell. You have to think about other people's feelings and not just about your own immediate gratification. It's this simple: either a guy is available and you can consider him or he's taken and you have nothing to do with him. You have a life of your own and you should never be someone's reserve option. Remember, if he cheats on them, he'll cheat on you.

It's a rebound thing.
Rebounds will only make you feel worse about your break up. If you've recently come out of a relationship, you're just not ready for anything serious. I dated AJ to get over my ex, J, and it really didn't work. We were seeing each other for six weeks and I felt physically sick when I had sex with him. It was just the ego boost I needed, but I never felt any butterflies when I saw him. Honestly, it just made me miss J, not ideal.

GUYS TO AVOID

Let's face it, you can't actually change someone. If you are playing a player, games are only a short-term solution, even if you get seriously good at it. Players don't become monogamous men.

Look at my ex S. Yes, I did get him to come running back after he told me he didn't want a relationship, but that didn't mean he was going to be faithful to me. I should have just accepted what he wanted and never looked back. It's pretty obvious, there are some guys that no amount of games are going to change. Avoid these guys at all costs, it's not worth your time or heartache.

The Unchangeables

The player
- He calls you pet names like 'sweetie' and 'hun', so he doesn't mix up your name with other girls
- He always has his phone on silent and never leaves it unattended
- He chases you and then backs off when he gets what he wants
- He has a wandering eye

The narcissist
- He thinks he can do no wrong
- He thinks he's always in the right
- He thinks he's the most important person in the room
- He cares about himself way more than anyone else

The attachment-issues guy
- He only wants to see you late at night
- He won't introduce you to his friends or family
- He is busy at the weekends
- He avoids the topic of whether you are official and makes you feel crazy for asking

The not-that-bothered guy
- He never takes you out on a date
- He always expects you to come to his place
- He doesn't make any effort during sex
- He isn't interested in getting to know you

The possessive guy
- He checks your phone and your emails
- He calls you and texts you repeatedly when you are apart
- He tells you what to wear
- He obsessively asks about your ex-boyfriends

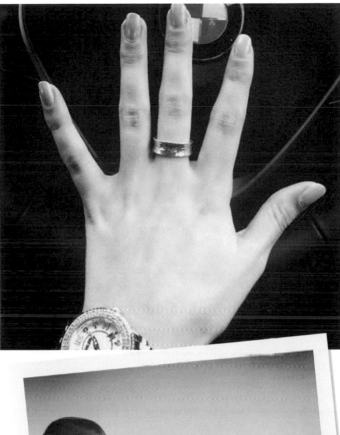

3

THE FIRST DATE

THE FIRST DATE RULES

Before the date

Go for drinks, not supper.
Organise to go for a drink first. If you are getting on well, then go for supper. You don't want to rock up to a restaurant and have to endure hours of awkwardness till the bill arrives. So, always do a test drink first.

Try to keep yourself busy.
Otherwise you'll totally overthink it. Try to distract yourself as much as possible beforehand.

Look good without overdoing it.
Although kind of obvious, it will massively boost your confidence. On a first date I would wear jeans, or smart trousers, with a cool top and heels. You want him to be looking at your face not staring at your body. He can discover the rest of you as time goes on.

It's either legs or boobs.
Show off your best assets but not at the same time. Yes, you will get guys if you dress provocatively, but they'll be the kind of guys who are only after one thing…

Smell good.
Pack your handbag with perfume and mints.
It's scientifically proven that scent stimulates
a man's attraction. Smell good, but don't drown
yourself in it.

Don't wear lots of make-up on a first date.
You don't want to start off wearing lots of make-
up, and then gradually pare it back, date by date,
because eventually he will wake up to you, and
be like, who the hell are you? If looking natural
isn't good enough for him, then he isn't even
vaguely good enough for you. End of.

Don't wear a bright lipstick on a date.
Just in case you want to kiss him, you don't
want the awkwardness of having to wipe it off
your face. Or worse getting it all over your teeth.

Plan an escape route.
Just in case. I always make a plan with one
of my friends to call me with an escape route
during the date. I can then choose whether I
take it up or not! But make sure you have some
phone signal. Basements mean zero signal and
zero escape route.

Don't turn up drunk.
Obviously!

During the date

Maintain eye contact.
Not in a creepy way. But in a sexy I-am-not-intimidated-or-nervous way.

Laugh a lot.
It will calm your nerves and will make you appear easy-going and relaxed.

Listen and don't talk about yourself all the time.
No one likes narcissistic behaviour.
Ask questions but don't interview him.
Return questions with questions. Take an interest.

Don't speak with your mouth full.
No one wants to see that.

Don't tell him your life story.
Or a complete account of your childhood. It's not that interesting and definitely isn't sexy. If you really need to speak about it that night, call your mum afterwards.

Don't describe your bad points.
Everyone has them – I'm fussy, too honest sometimes, not very friendly, I get into bad moods easily, especially if I'm hungry or tired.

But a guy doesn't need to know this. Remember, you have only just met him.

Keep any weird habits to yourself.
It's a turn-off to come across as mega fussy or difficult. We all have them, but keep them to yourself, remember its TMI (too much information) for a first date.

Never talk about your ex-boyfriends.
It will immediately put a guy off, keep your issues to yourself he isn't your therapist or your girlfriend. If he specifically asks you what happened in your last relationship, answer, but keep it seriously minimal.

Don't get drunk.
Falling over or slurring aren't and never will be cute.

Offer to pay for something on the first date.
It speaks a lot about your views on equality. If he insists on picking up the bill, then he is a gentleman. If he suggests you split the bill, it's not totally ideal but it's not a deal breaker. If he lets you pay for the meal, don't date him again. If you let him pay for you all the time, he's inclined to see you as a possession and will not treat you as an equal. You don't want to take a guy's balls away from him, but at the same time maintain

TRUST IS LIKE AN

ERASER.

IT GETS SMALLER AND
SMALLER AFTER EVERY

MISTAKE.

your independence, insist on paying for the occasional drink, or taxi ride.

Don't kiss on the first date.
It will leave him wanting more. If you really can't hold out, make sure it's not in some dark corner of a nightclub, because that's just rank and really doesn't say 'I respect myself – so respect me'. Kiss on the second or third date.

Never sleep with him on the first date.
If you do, he'll think you are easy. If you want to play the game, hold out for a while because it will make him want you more. Every guy wants what he can't have. Never let a guy pressure you into having sex. If he likes you, he will wait. There is no timescale for when you should sleep with him as everyone is different. It could be on the third date, or even after a couple of months, but just never, ever on the first.

Second & third dates
So the awkward first date has been and gone. The second and third dates are much easier. As you know a bit more about each other and you're both still interested, so the pressure is off. Go to the cinema (or something casual), where you can actually enjoy hanging out together and then if you want, go for drinks afterwards.

Be slightly more tactile.
Not over the top, but if you do like him, casual flirting is acceptable.

Work out if he is your kind of guy.
Are you attracted to him? Does he make you laugh? Do you have chemistry?

...If he is.
Don't make it too obvious. Keep him guessing.

If he makes the first move, kiss him.
Not too intimately, leave something up to his imagination.

Don't invite him over to your place or go to his.
It's too invasive. Taxi.

Don't sleep with him.
It's still too soon and even if you feel you know him really well by this stage, you don't. You've only met the guy three times!

★ The 5 Rules ★

1. Try to keep busy before the date
2. Is he interested and interesting?
3. Don't overshare
4. Don't talk about your ex or other 'issues'
5. Never have sex on the first date

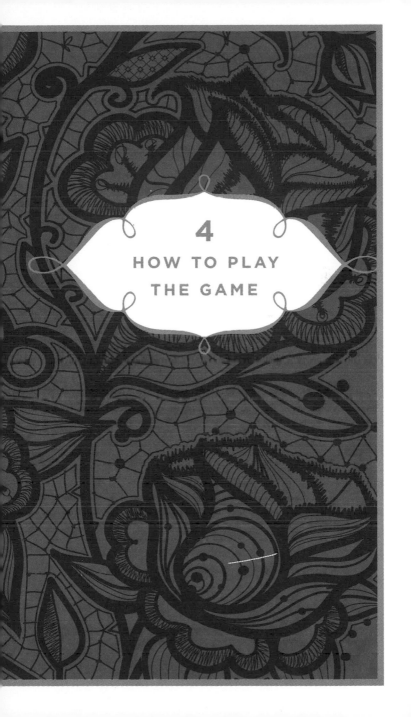

4

HOW TO PLAY
THE GAME

So you've been on a couple of dates and you've started to kind of like him, don't get too comfortable yet. If you've ever found yourself analysing everrry message in your conversation history for clues as to why he hasn't texted you back, or you've drunk dialled a guy because you thought he would just really love to hear from you, at like 3 a.m – think again. The dating game rules mean you can't start doing whatever you want, just because you like the guy. Play the game.

When I first started dating S, I found out that he was still sleeping with other girls. I told him I found it completely disgusting and that if he was sleeping with me, he should not be sleeping with other people. I told him I was an all-or-nothing girl, so we were nothing. I was never going to be a doormat – sitting around waiting for him to decide if he wanted to date me exclusively. Come on. So I played the game. Or more exactly, I played him at his own game. I dated other guys and made sure S knew about it. I flirted with A, and dangled him in front of S. I wanted him to know that he wasn't the only one who could do whatever he wanted. It made S want me even more. He quickly realised that although it was fine for him to play the field, it didn't feel quite so cool when the girl he liked played him at his

Follow Your Heart But Take Your Brain With You.

own game. Lesson taught. Sometimes, you just need to make guys realise they need to stick to your rules.

Don't ever feel bad about playing a guy, it's the whole point of the dating game; they do it to us all the time, and it is empowering to be in control. Men are used to girls being keen, especially once they've slept with them. Don't be that needy girl who texts and calls all the time. Play them at their own game and make them run after you.

The dating game is an attitude that enables you to feel in control and have equal dating power. Obviously, not all guys are players and will treat you badly, but you can make sure that each guy will fall for you because, unlike the other girls, you will keep him on his toes.

THE RULES FOR TEXTING & EMAILING

Keep texting brief.
Never reveal too much at this early stage. Guys don't need to know your social calendar or what you've had for breakfast.

Don't reply to text messages straight away.
I like to keep guys waiting. If he texts during the day – you're busy. Leave it a while. If he sends you a text without any questions, then don't reply. The conversation doesn't have to end with you.

Never text more than twice in a row.
The most you can say, if you really, really, really have to is: 'Oi'. That way you, at least are taking control and not letting him walk all over you. If he doesn't reply to that, never text him again.

Don't Whatsapp or BBM.
That 'last-seen-at' message will drive you crazy, as you will constantly know if he has read your message and not replied. Plus, he really shouldn't know when you have read his messages. It's too open. Don't make contact that easy for him.

Don't 'sext' or drunk text.
Both of these come across as desperate. If you can't help yourself, don't take your phone out on a night out. Or delete his number. Or both.

If he texts you before you go to sleep.
Reply. You don't want to play too many games. As that's all you will get in return.

Text him and then don't reply.
Why not, keep him on his toes! I often used to text JL, and then never reply when he texted me back. It left him totally confused. Sometimes I didn't reply to any of his texts, even though he knew I was reading them. I'd eventually get back to him saying something like 'sorry for late reply, I've been really busy.' When actually I'd just been at home playing with my dog. Keep them guessing.

THE RULES FOR PHONE CALLS

Don't always pick up your phone.
If you were at home the last time he called, don't be at home again. You don't want him to think you're waiting around for your next date, you want him to think you are busy and have other things going on. So, the next time he calls, don't pick up. Reply with a text saying you've got bad signal, are with someone or are working. You shouldn't be contactable at all hours. You aren't a loser waiting by your phone.

Don't talk for hours.
He isn't your best friend and you want to get to know each other properly face to face. So don't give him a blow-by-blow account of your gym

routine, keep it short and simple and always end phone calls first.

Don't drunk dial.
Whatever you say will not be good, even if you convince yourself that you really have to speak to him as it's a genius idea. It's not and you really don't. Call a friend. Tell anyone. Call anyone, but don't call him.

Don't leave answerphone messages.
Unless you really have to. He will return your missed call when he gets it. No need for the seriously awkward message… "Hi it's just me… wondered what you were up to. Wait, sorry I didn't say who I am. Never mind. Bye". You know the ones.

Don't leave him more than one missed call.
Two is too many, twenty is scary.

THE RULES FOR FACEBOOK, INSTAGRAM, TWITTER & SNAPCHAT

Don't add him.
Ideally, let him find you and add you. The rules of the chase apply to social media too.

Don't change your status before or after a date.
He will eventually see and be freaked out.

Don't like his Facebook statuses and profile pictures.
It's stalker-ish and way too early to start putting your name all over his wall.

Don't contact him via another social site if he hasn't texted you back.
He'll know what you are doing. Just wait; if you're feeling impatient, find something else to do. Quit obsessing.

Don't like every Instagram picture he puts up.
Again, it's bordering on looking waaay too interested. Remember, you have other things going on, you don't have time to look, let alone like his pictures.

Don't poke him on Facebook.
He'll think it's some kind of booty call.

Don't add his friends on Facebook.
You're being too keen, too soon.

Don't be in a relationship on Facebook.
In fact, remove your relationship status, no one needs constant updates on your private life. Hide it from your profile.

Wait for him to put a photo of you on Instagram before you put one up of him.
Let him make the first show of commitment. But, you may be waiting years...

FURTHER DATING GAME RULES

Don't accept last-minute weekend dates.
He needs to book it in advance. You are busy. Obviously.

Never cancel plans if they conflict with a date.
You have your own life. Hoes before bros, honey.

Always keep him waiting 5-10 minutes.
I was meant to be meeting JL for dinner at 8.30 p.m. I rang beforehand, to warn him to be on time. And I left my house at 8.20 p.m. He called five minutes later, frantically wondering where I was. I told him I was nearly there. After getting over his initial annoyance, JL spent the rest of the evening trying to please me. If you accidentally turn up early, go round the block or make a phone call.

Don't be too available.
If you are always available, it's just plain unattractive, remember a guy needs the thrill of the chase. Even if you aren't busy, act like you are. If he asks you out without enough notice,

say no, he needs to know you have a life outside of dating him. I've made all these mistakes, so you don't have to. When I was with my first boyfriend, H, I would keep every weekend free, just in case he decided he wanted to do something. Not a good look. Have a life of your own.

Change your date.
Guys think their date with you, will be the highlight of your week. If you rearrange your date, to a different day (one that is just that bit more convenient for you), it will leave them confused, wondering what could be more important?

THE RULES FOR SEX

Don't rush your first time.
I want to be very clear, you should never feel pressurised into losing your virginity because you want to please your boyfriend or keep up with your friends. Make sure you are in a secure relationship and you feel completely comfortable. It's an important moment and you will never get it back. I don't regret my first time, it was with someone I liked a lot and felt really safe with. I had been dating him for a couple of months. My friend was dating his best friend and we ended up losing our virginities on the same night – quite sad really! We used a condom, I made sure of that. Everyone's

'right' time is different. You, and only you, know when it is right.

First time with a guy.
Around a month is always a smart period to wait, as even the most hardened player will probably have given up the chase before this stage. If you want to get rid of the players, wait.

Don't feel pressured into having sex.
Usually, guys want to have sex as soon as possible. Sex just doesn't have quite the same impact on guys as it has on girls. So, even if a guy tries his luck, you need to work out if you feel ready. Don't worry about a guy losing interest. If he does, then he can get lost. He's not even vaguely good enough for you.

Bad first-time sex.
Generally, the first time isn't mind-blowing or even that great. Don't necessarily think this is a bad sign. You are probably both nervous and don't know what each other wants.

Protect yourself.
Be smart, use a condom. You don't know his previous sexual history. Unprotected sex is not a good look. I don't care if he says it doesn't feel good. If he respects you, he should use protection. Every time.

Don't let him stay over.
Even if you have had sex. It confuses him. As
soon as you let a guy sleep in your bed, you are
exposing yourself at your most vulnerable. If you
aren't ready, don't let him stay over. Sleeping in
bed with someone is often more intimate than
sex. If you aren't ready, you aren't ready. Girls
are always stereotyped as intimately more needy,
wanting a guy to cuddle them, and stay over
after sex. A lot of guys actually like this too,
so if you do the unexpected, and not let him
sleep over, he will go home and think about you
all night.

While I was dating JL, I would never let him
sleep in my bed. He'd be at mine and we may
have got a bit drunk and then he'd ask to stay
over and I would tell him to leave. He'd act
completely confused and ask what I meant,
thinking he was obviously staying the night.
I'd ask him which of us was going to sleep in
my flatmate's bed. Once, I even kicked JL out
after we had sex. I just showed him the door. He
left in a mood, but then texted me five minutes
later, pretending he had left his keys at mine.
Seriously? I told him to get them in the morning.
I didn't want him to come back to mine because
I knew he would find a way of staying. The truth
was I didn't want to expose my vulnerability, I
knew it would hurt me, so I didn't let him get too
close to me.

Don't date a guy who is selfish in bed.
It will mean he is selfish in general. I've dated guys who are selfish in bed before and it has always reflected their attitude during the relationship. Sex is about giving and receiving, which will ultimately strengthen your relationship, so don't date anyone who only wants to please themselves. Seriously!

Don't date a guy who plays games.
In the long term, you do want to let your guard down and you don't want a relationship based around point scoring.

★ The 5 Rules ★

1. Keep texts short
2. Don't be available all the time
3. Don't accept a weekend date without enough warning
4. Sleep with him when you are ready
5. Be smart, use protection

5

HE'S JUST NOT *THAT* INTERESTED

A LOT OF GIRLS WASTE TIME ON GUYS who aren't *that* into them. They don't want to see the truth and ignore all the warning signs. Don't be that girl. Move on. If he's not that into you, don't hang out with him any more; don't try to make him date you. Don't let him waste your time. If he's not that into you, find someone who is.

I speak from experience here. I was a tiny bit too obsessed with my second boyfriend, J, and I ignored all the signs that he wasn't that interested because I wanted to make it work. I fell for J hard. Looking back, I think it was because he was a little bit older and just seemed to be more mature than the other guys I'd dated. But, just like S, he had recently come out of a long-term relationship, and warned me that he wasn't ready for a girlfriend. I thought I could change that (yes, major error). So, I kept on waiting, hoping that if I just kept holding on he would eventually change...which never happened. Obviously.

J's behaviour throughout was far from ideal; from saying he didn't want to be friends on Facebook, as it seemed too 'serious', to going on benders with his friends and not contacting me for days on end, without any excuse when

he eventually bothered to get back in touch. As I write this, I really can't believe the excuses I made for some of the things that happened during our relationship. Which ultimately allowed him to carry on treating me however he wanted. I should have walked.

The worst by far was when J went to Vegas on holiday and broke up with me in a drunken text. I couldn't accept it and begged him to stay with me. I then went to my mum's house and literally cried non-stop. After three days of silence, J texted me with a picture of his new tattoo on his butt cheek (1 know, alarm bells), explaining he had been on a drunken rampage for the last five days and that he didn't know what he'd been doing or saying, and asked if we were ok. I replied instantly saying it was fine and that I hoped he was having a really nice time, as though nothing was wrong. What the hell? I was obsessed with him, obsessed! Please learn from my mistakes – I would never let this happen again. And hopefully, now neither will you.

Learn to recognise the signs, the sooner you do, the less involved you will be and the less of your time is wasted. Drop him. Move on.

THE BIG IFS

If he's not texting you, or calling you.
Obviously! There is nothing you can do, other
than look desperate and needy if you contact
him repeatedly.

If he's only ringing you at night.
He's clearly only interested in sex. Delete him.

If he's texting other girls while he is with you.
Could there be a more obvious red flag?
J once sent me a text just before he went out:

J: Night, sleep well, x

J: Where are you? (one minute later)

ME: You just text me, I'm in bed.

J: Sorry, I meant to say, what have you eaten?

ME: What are you talking about?

That typo text clearly wasn't meant for me, so I
demanded that he tell me who he had actually
meant to text. He couldn't justify himself. I
didn't speak to him for two days. What I should
have done was finish with him, but I fell for
his excuses, because I wanted to believe them.

I didn't want to admit to myself that he wasn't committed to me and never would be.

If you over analyse every message.
I used to ring my friends after every text J sent me. Asking, how do I reply? How long do I take to respond? Because I never felt sure that I was enough to keep him interested. My friends were seriously supportive, but after the whole Vegas thing, they got a bit sick and tired of hearing about it, because whatever happened I kept on forgiving him and they could only tolerate so much. Don't bore your friends – yes, your friends should always be there for you, but don't abuse them. If your friends are getting tired of your relationship issues, then your relationship is probably not working.

If he only wants to see you twice a week.
And you've been together for months. Sure, see each other once or twice at the beginning, but things should progress. If that natural progression doesn't happen, I'm sorry, it's never going to happen.

If he never spends the weekends with you.
Don't make excuses for him, the truth is he would just rather spend his weekend with other people. Be brutally honest with yourself, he's taking you for granted.

If he's not introducing you to his parents.
J would make plans to introduce me to his mum,
but then cancel them every time. He knew our
relationship wasn't going anywhere, so he didn't
want me to meet her. It was that simple.

If he's not introducing you to his friends.
One of my exes used to keep me entirely separate
from his friends. He used to go out with them,
then separately, take me out. We were kept apart.
If you aren't spending time with his friends,
then it's because he doesn't want you getting too
involved in his life and he isn't proud enough of
you. In short, he is taking you for a ride.

If he's not involving you in his life.
It's very obvious when he's not investing his
time and energy into making it work. Don't try
to compensate and make up for his lack of effort.
Girls often try too hard to make things right.
Honestly, at this stage, he should be doing all
the running.

If he only uses the term 'seeing each other'.
If he liked you enough he would make it exclusive
and official. Don't be fooled by the term 'seeing
each other', if you aren't dating anyone else, then
nor should he. The term 'seeing each other' leaves
far too many grey areas in the relationship, which
both of you can interpret differently. Boundaries
are there for a reason.

If he doesn't want to make it official.
'I just don't want to put a label on it' or 'I don't like the words girlfriend, boyfriend, they're really unnecessary'. They're completely necessary! Don't let anyone make you think that they're not.

If he tells you he doesn't want a girlfriend.
Unfortunately, if he tells you he doesn't want a relationship, he doesn't. There is nothing you can do to change it. Yes, you can make him want and desire you, but it won't ever give you a successful relationship.

If you are making excuses for him.
I made a lot of excuses for J and other guys before him. There are a lot of excuses you can make for someone you like, but ultimately, if it's right it's right, if it's wrong it's wrong. Stop making excuses for him.

If he doesn't try to impress you.
If he makes no effort to impress you with any kind of gesture, whether it's taking you out to dinner or just picking you up from your home. He's just not that interested.

If you are just not that into him...

Sometimes feelings can develop, but generally, you'll instinctively know if you like him and want to take things further. There is no point in pushing yourself into something, when it doesn't feel right from the beginning. Trust your instincts. If you feel any of the 'ifs' in this chapter about him, then you are just not that into him.

Keep your options open.

If you aren't sure about him and not convinced if he's that that into you, but you want to give it a bit of time, make sure you keep your eyes open – don't limit your options!

 ★ **The 5 Rules** ★

1. He rarely gets in touch
2. He only calls you late at night
3. He doesn't introduce you to his family or friends
4. You keep on having to make excuses for him
5. He tells you he doesn't want a girlfriend

6
RELATIONSHIP
RULES

S O YOU ARE OFFICIALLY TOGETHER. Welcome to a relationship status. Maybe things have got a bit more serious or you've started to spend more time together. Either way, you'll still need the dating game rules. You have to keep the spark alive and not rush into things. Don't sprint like some world-class athlete to the next stage of a relationship. Breathe and take things slowly.

I've had a couple of whirlwind relationships that I definitely didn't take slowly enough. The problem with whirlwinds is that they pick you up and take you very high, but then drop you very hard. My relationship with S is a prime example of this, as it moved way too quickly. One minute we had just started dating, the next we were on our first holiday together in Barcelona and then S had told me he loved me and wanted to give me keys to his flat. I knew it was all too soon and I told him that it was freaking me out. But he just turned around and told me that he thought I was actually quite excited by it. He explained that he wanted me to trust him, as I was different to any other girl he had ever met and wanted me to feel as though I could go to his place without even calling him first. I thought, how sweet, he really is trying. Maybe he was

I'D AGREE
WITH YOU
BUT THEN
WE'D
BOTH BE
WRONG

right? Maybe I wasn't really freaked out and actually wanted it too? We spent almost every night together for two months. I practically moved into his flat.

Looking back, I shouldn't have let S rush me and we should have taken things a bit slower. Don't get me wrong, nothing would have stopped S from cheating on me, because that's just his and his therapist's problem. But if I had followed the dating game rules, I would never have been with him in the first place because he was a serial cheater. And if I had followed the relationship rules, I would have been much more prepared for what happened, as I wouldn't have been anywhere near as attached as I was.

Ultimately, your life can't revolve around your relationship – I've made this mistake numerous times – yes, you love that person; yes, you want to spend all your time with them; yes, you really enjoy his company. But you can't make your boyfriend the centre of your universe. You need to keep a balance between spending time with your boyfriend and spending time with your friends, family and work. Otherwise your relationship will become claustrophobic and way too intense. You need to try and give each other space while still being together.

THE RULES FOR YOUR RELATIONSHIP

Keep your social life.
At the start of a relationship, you should see him twice a week. However, as time goes on, you may reach a point where you are sleeping with him every other night, but that doesn't mean you can't still go to dinner or party with your friends.

Still go on dates.
Once a week you should make time to go out with each other. It's an opportunity to dress up and go out and remember exactly why you make each other happy. It also makes you look and feel good, and he gets to show you off. It beats sitting in every night together.

Socialise with each other.
It's important to go out separately, but it's also important to go out together with each other's friends. Going out or hanging out with other people strengthens a relationship. It's too much pressure on both of you, if you only spend time with each other exclusively.

Have a passion outside of your relationship.
Have a passion or hobby outside of your

relationship. If you don't have one, find one. If you don't enjoy your job or your studies, it's good to have something else you are interested in. I love horse riding and if I ever need to clear my head, I go riding. If I feel stressed-out, I go to the gym to burn off my stress. If you aren't confident enough to join a club by yourself, find something fun to do with your friends.

Be realistic.
A lot of girls think their boyfriends can do no wrong. It's important to keep things in perspective, your boyfriend isn't perfect but, hey, no one is. Don't put him on a pedestal. It isn't fair on him or you. Nobody is perfect; we're all a bit weird. Get to know each other's weirdness.

Remember there are ups and downs.
Neither of you can be perfect all the time, you will get stressed out with each other. Don't freak out if you aren't a perfect couple all the time, accept that you both have flaws. The most important thing; is to try and make each other happy as much and as often as you can.

Don't become needy.
You survived just fine before the relationship started, so you don't need him to support you or help you make every decision now. Come on, what happened to girl power?

Speak your mind.
Don't be afraid of speaking your mind in case
you damage your relationship. Always agreeing
and saying yes isn't attractive. You don't want
to be a pushover and a relationship involves two
people. Not one.

Don't ditch your friends.
Girls are particularly bad at forgetting about
their friends when they have fallen for a guy.
They go for a year and a half of spending all
their time with their boyfriend, then it goes tits
up, and they don't have any friends left. Don't
make that mistake.

**...And let your boyfriend have time with his
friends.**
Be supportive and even encourage him to spend
time with his guys. His friends will respect you
and he will enjoy your time together more if he
gets to have his guy time.

Make plans.
The daily grind can get you both down. Plan
adventurous things to do together. Going to
new places and exploring new things is one
of the greatest things about being in a
relationship. If you feel ready, definitely plan a
mini-break or holiday with your boyfriend.

I remember it was during a supper in Barcelona with S that he then turned to me and told me he could see himself falling in love with me, it was all pretty romantic. S and I travelled a lot when we were together, we even went to Cannes during the film festival. And yes, it didn't end very well, but it doesn't mean that the memories aren't pretty great.

Don't be desperate to rush into things.
Moving in together, getting engaged and even married are all massive life-changing steps. Don't sprint towards them like it's some kind of crazy race. Try to enjoy the process rather than constantly wanting to get to the next stage. You need to know someone extremely well before getting more serious. I think it's really important to live with your boyfriend before even thinking about taking the next step, because living together full-time is very different to spending a lot of time someone.

Keep your own life.
Have other things going on. Remember he is a part but not the whole of your life.

Don't let yourself go.
Don't get super relaxed just because you feel
comfortable in a relationship. Don't stop wearing
make-up, plucking your eyebrows, wearing cool
clothes or going to the gym. Don't start eating all
the junk food your boyfriend does and piling on
the pounds: yes, we all know those boyfriend-is-
to-blame pounds. Obviously, it's much easier for
some girls to stay skinnier than others, but it's
not about being skinny, it's about taking pride
in your appearance, for your own happiness.
If you have made an effort, people can tell and
it's attractive. As long as you make the best of
what you've got, you can feel super confident and
happy knowing you are the best version of you.

Don't be afraid to let him see the real you.
I used to go to huge lengths to make H believe I
had long hair. I'd go to bed with my extensions in
and then I'd quietly unclip them, slide them out
and off the side of the bed before he noticed. I'd
tie up my remaining hair so he didn't find out.
As soon as I woke up the next morning, I'd
quickly bundle my extensions underneath my
vest and run to the loo to put them back in.
Obviously, I couldn't sustain that amount of
effort and had to come clean eventually. The
same goes for wearing chicken fillets in your
bra. As far as I'm concerned, chicken fillets or

a massively padded bra are false advertising.
If you don't have big boobs, you have just got to
own up to it, because your boyfriend will find out
eventually, like when you get naked! The real
you is the one he likes, don't feel you have to
pretend to be someone you are not.

Be yourself.
Don't try to be the person he wants you to be or
the person you think you should be. Be yourself.
You will break sooner or later. If your boyfriend
doesn't want to see you in your granny pants,
when you are on your period or when you are
mortally hungover, then he doesn't care that
much. He isn't freaking perfect and you don't
have to be all the time. Love should be a little bit
more unconditional than having to be on the best
form all of the time.

THE RULES FOR LOVE

Are you in love?
Falling in love is one of the strongest feelings
out there; it completely engulfs you. It feels as
though the two of you are the only people in the
world; it's as though you have an invisible rope
attaching you to the other person. It makes you
laugh, it makes you feel dizzy, it makes you feel
untouchable and, yes, sometimes it makes you
cry. It's unmistakeable.

WHEN PEOPLE TELL ME "YOU'RE GONNA REGRET THAT IN THE MORNING" I SLEEP IN UNTIL NOON BECAUSE I'M A PROBLEM SOLVER.

When to say 'I love you'.
It doesn't really matter who is the first one to say it, unless it has been like a week, then hold those words in, lady. I prefer that it is said to me first and although it always has been that way, we are all grown-ups and if you think the time is right – then you should say it. There is no equation for when to say those three words, it's not maths. Just don't say it on your second date...

Do you have to say I love you back?
If you aren't sure that you are in love with him, then you definitely don't have to say it back. It's not rude. You just aren't there yet. Don't stress. It will come and you will know when you do. Don't force it.

THE RULES FOR GREAT SEX

Be open about what you like.
If there is something you aren't enjoying when you have sex, let him know. It's not all about him. When you are in a relationship, it's nice to figure out what works for both of you and talk openly about what turns you on, in an undemanding way. I'm very much a person who believes honesty is the best policy, especially with sex. The more honest you are, the better the sex is. You don't want a guy to be doing something to you that you really don't like, because he thinks

you do, and in fact you are just hoping he will stop. Come on. Sex is about pleasure not pain.

Never fake an orgasm.
Yes, we all do it. But seriously, why? I have faked it a lot in the past. I had to watch a lot of porn to learn those skills! But it got to a stage, with one of my exes, when I hadn't orgasmed once from sex in six months and I couldn't keep faking. So I told him. Awkward! It was not only a massive hit to his confidence, but we had to start from scratch, and it could have been so easily avoided if I had just been honest. Dating game lesson learnt. You should never fake it. Yes, it can sometimes be demoralising for him. But make sure you let him know that you do really enjoy sex, but you just haven't orgasmed yet and you want to try to figure out how to get there, together. It then becomes a bit of a challenge for him, and guys actually quite like a challenge in the bedroom.

Special occasions.
On birthdays and Valentine's day you should definitely try new things. Don't be afraid of experimenting with your boyfriend to find out what turns you both on. I once gave an ex a blow job book as a Valentine's present. I told him he could pick two that he would like me to do to him. One of them was called 'The Ice Cube' and the other was called 'The Goddess', where I had

to act completely over the top, flicking my hair all over the shop. Sex doesn't have to be serious. It's about having fun.

Wear something cute to bed.
You don't want to sleep naked with your boyfriend, otherwise you'll be constantly hassled for sex. At the same time, it's not exactly seductive if you wear your pyjamas all the time. Wear a vest top and shorts and if you want to rock a sexier look, go out and buy something seriously hot to surprise him with.

Change it up.
Don't get stuck in a routine. Try different types of foreplay and change positions. Or even play with food or toys. I've never tried bondage, because I think it's a bit freaky, but if your boyfriend is into it, then maybe you should try it? Definitely experiment and mix things up, but don't force yourself to do anything you feel uncomfortable with.

Let him pleasure you.
A lot of us find it difficult to let ourselves be pleasured during sex. Be selfish, sex is too often centred around a guy. Make yourself the focus.

Let go of your inhibitions.
Experiment. Have sex outside. The fear of getting caught is a massive turn on. There are so

In life you will meet
two kinds of people.
Ones who *build*
you up, and ones
who *tear* you down.
But in the end, you
will *thank* them both

many places to try, the shower, a park or even in the sea. But not in a nightclub, I think that's just a bit gross. I've had sex in loads of different places. I've even had sex on a hay bale once. I wouldn't recommend that one, it's not ideal comfort-wise but, hey, go and experiment!

Dress up.
Dressing up is seriously seductive. If I hadn't seen J for a couple of days, I would surprise him with a kinky outfit. I once lay on his bed wearing a full policewoman's outfit (hat and badge included).

Regular sex.
Sex is an essential part of a healthy relationship. If you haven't had sex for a while, remember that everyone goes through dry patches. Just make sure you talk about it, so it doesn't become something you can never bring up.

★ The 5 Rules ★

1. Have your own life
2. Keep going on dates with each other
3. Tell him what you like in bed
4. Don't ditch your friends
5. Make plans together

7

THE FAMILY, FRIENDS & EX FACTOR

THERE ARE ONLY TWO PEOPLE in a relationship. But when you include the opinions of friends and family, it can start to feel as though there are way more people involved. That doesn't even begin to cover meeting his family, getting on with his friends, introducing him to your family and friends, how your friends react to him, your relationship with your friends and his ex-girlfriends coming out of the woodwork… To be honest, it can all get pretty overwhelming!

Being in a relationship just isn't as simple as 'you and him'. It's also about meeting the people in each other's lives. It's kind of simple – but guidelines are needed. As let's be honest, there's nothing worse than being unprepared for awkward situations.

MEETING HIS FAMILY

Find out the do's and don't's.
Ask your boyfriend about everything that you can and can't say before you meet his parents. Find out what their personalities are like and what subjects are no-go areas. Work it out beforehand so you don't have to face any painfully long, awkward silences.

Focus on his mum.
It works every time. They are the ones you need to make a real connection with. Make your boyfriend's mum like you and it'll make your life so much easier. S was a real mummy's boy, but she could never get hold of him, so I became her first port of call.

Don't show any cleavage or wear anything revealing.
I don't think I even need to explain why this is a seriously bad idea! Sure, look your best, but not in that way!

Be as unthreatening as possible.
Respect that they may be protective of him, so don't go in way too overconfident trying to prove how great you are and how ideal you would be as a future daughter-in-law. It's not a job interview. Don't ask them about their family medical history. Just make light conversation!

Say good things about your boyfriend.
Obviously. They want to know you care.

Never be rude about their son.
In any shape or form. Don't list your criticisms of them or bang on about their bad points. It will never go down well.

MEETING HIS FRIENDS

Hanging out with your boyfriend's friends is crucial. If you don't get on with them, it can put a serious strain on your relationship. His friends are his extended family and they are going to be the people he'll turn to when he has an argument with you. Make sure you have them on side.

Use it as an opportunity to make more friends.
Try to get to know them. You get on with your boyfriend, so you'll no doubt also get on with his friends.

Laugh at yourself.
Let them wind you up, without getting uptight. J's friends used to take the piss out of me because I rarely drink alcohol. I laughed it off and carried on doing my thing.

Never flirt with your boyfriend's friends.
You've got to control yourself. I have fancied quite a few of my boyfriend's friends before. It's pretty easy as usually their attitude is really similar to your boyfriend's, but don't take it any further. This is serious no-go territory.

Don't text his friends or add them on Facebook.
If you've only just met them. You don't want to come across like a major try-hard.

Get your friends involved.
It's important to hang out in a group, not just one-on-one with your boyfriend's friends. It makes it way more fun and way less intense.

Use it as an opportunity to see how they react to you.
Make an effort with them and they should do the same back, if their friend cares about you. If they don't think their friend is that into you, they won't make much of an effort. I found it quite hard to hang out with J's friends. They were really awkward around me and they wouldn't make any conversation. I think it's because they knew J's heart wasn't in the relationship.

THE EX FACTOR

Frankly, I don't think it's acceptable for your boyfriend to stay friends with his ex, or for you, for that matter. It's inconsiderate, it's inappropriate and unnecessary. If you want to go forwards and have a future with someone, you have to leave your past behind. You don't need that person in your life, you don't need to hang out with him. You've got other friends. End of.

THE RULES FOR YOUR FRIENDSHIPS

Girls' friendships are incredibly close and sometimes get seriously damaged by guys, which is completely wrong. Friendships should always come before relationships, as trust me you will need your friends if your relationship hits the rocks. I've had quite a few bad experiences with 'so-called friends'. So I want to make it clear that there are some things that you should never, ever do to a friend and there are some girls who should never be your friends.

The Friendship Nevers

Never compete over a guy.
No guy is worth it. Don't date someone who makes you feel even slightly competitive with a friend. Your friendship should always come before any guy. True friendships should never be competitive.

Never have 'frenemies'.
Make sure you choose your friends wisely. Real friends are the ones you can trust with your life let alone with a guy. Real friends don't backstab you because of a guy. The girls that do are not your real friends. They are your 'frenemies'. (friend-enemies). I've been there and it's totally not worth it. When I first hooked-up with JL, he was completely within his rights to see whoever he wanted as we weren't exclusive. His friend, P,

didn't know about us when she went on a date with him. But when she did find out, instead of getting annoyed and telling him he was an idiot for seeing us both, she got really catty towards me. She suddenly tried to do whatever it would take to get him. I clearly told JL not to play us against each other, because it was wrong. The whole experience made me realise that she wasn't my kind of girl, and would never be my friend.

Never date a friend's ex-boyfriend.
It's too messy to involve yourself in their history and you could end up losing them both. I wouldn't want one of my best friends to date one of my exes; if I had been in love with them, it would hurt me waaay too much. Let's face it, it's never easy to see the boyfriend, who you once loved with someone else. But to see them with your friend is doubly hurtful. It comes down to loyalty. Friends before dates, ladies.

The exception to this rule is when you have only casually dated a guy. I dated A before he went out with my best friend, B. I didn't like A nearly enough to stand in the way of B's happiness when they fell for each other. But, history is history and pretty hard to erase, so if possible, I would avoid recycling any friends' ex-dates and obviously never go near ex-boyfriends.

Never hook up with your friend's boyfriend.
Hopefully, I don't even need to tell you this. It's
a given fact. All girls should know the difference
between right and wrong, and stealing your
friend's boyfriend is about as wrong as it gets.
But it's been done to me.

I met my best friend through my boyfriend at
the time, all the guys loved her. We immediately
became really close and we saw each other every
day. She was the one who I would turn to, if I fell
out with my boyfriend. She would always say
the right things. After I heard he had cheated
on me yet again, she was the one who was really
there for me. She took me out and told me I
would be fine.

It was her ex-boyfriend who broke the news to
me that she had been repeatedly having sex with
my boyfriend before we broke up. She denied it
and I believed her because I refused to accept
that any best friend could do that to me. But the
rumours wouldn't stop.

I decided there was only one way to find out – I
needed to speak to him. She was sitting next to
me in the car when I made the phone call. I was
so distraught that I burst into tears and begged
him to tell me the truth. He finally admitted
over loudspeaker that the rumours were true

and they had been sleeping together while we were together. The colour literally drained from her face and she started screaming that he was a liar. But I could tell from her body language that she was the one who was lying. I slammed on the brakes and told her to get out of my car. I dumped her on the side of the road and drove off. I've never seen her again. But I have found out that they are together. I can't imagine it will last, as it's a relationship based on cheating and lies.

I was so miserable for a while. I would cry down the phone to my mum and tell her I wanted to die. I know it sounds dramatic, but I did. First love and first betrayals hurt like hell. I really couldn't understand how someone who loved me, could do that to me, and how one of my best friends could betray me like that. Obviously, not everyone will have experiences as bad as mine, and I'm not telling you not to trust your friends, but just choose them carefully. And, never do that to a friend.

Never ignore your friend's advice.
If my friends are saying something about my relationship, and it's upsetting me, then I know deep down that they are right. It's a hard reality to face, but you can't ignore it. Sometimes, your friends know you better than you know yourself, so trust their advice. Even if it hurts to hear it.

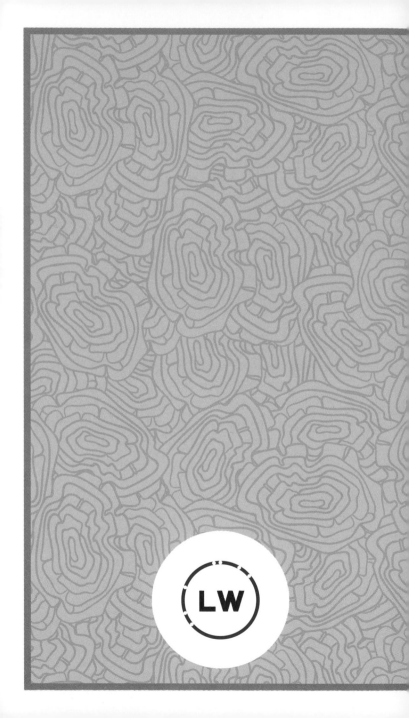

8

IS IT REALLY
WORKING?

IF YOU OFTEN ASK YOURSELF this question, then the chances are, it's not. It's now up to you to figure out what is going wrong and if you can fix it, or if it's time to accept that he's not quite the one. Sadly, a lot of girls stay in relationships because they are afraid of being alone and end up in a no-exit situation. Don't waste your time in a relationship that isn't working. I know it's tough, but you have to be strong, grow some balls, find the right guy, and not stick it out with the wrong one.

I've reached a point in a couple of relationships where I've known it was no longer working, but I've persuaded myself not to give up. Sometimes it's because I felt deep down there was something worth fighting for, and other times I have been too scared to turn around finally and end things. So I make a list. Yes it sounds dated, but it's impossible to think clearly when your head's a complete mess. Get it out of your head and onto paper. Make a list of the pros and cons, and write down what's working and what's not in your relationship. You have to be honest. Positives could be: I'm attracted to him, he makes me laugh, he gets on with my friends, he's generous, he's ambitious. Negatives could be: he puts me down, I don't trust him, he doesn't include me in his life. I'm not going to lie to you,

the process can be quite emotional, because you are forcing yourself to come to terms with the issues in your relationship. Some of which you may not be able to overcome. It's sad, as yes you have made an investment in that person and it's hard starting all over again but if you can't put up with them now, you wouldn't want to put up with them for the rest of your life.

I've made lists for all my ex-boyfriends – except S, there wasn't enough time, he had been cheating and that doesn't need a list, that's just over.

IS IT ACTUALLY WORKING?

80:20 ratio.
Ideally, you should be happy most of the time in a relationship. But realistically, no relationship is perfect and there are always rough patches. The good times should outweigh the bad though. I think the perfect relationship ratio is 80:20. If you spend more than 30 per cent of your relationship miserable, then you have to seriously think if you want to spend a third or more of your life unhappy. Is your relationship worth that much?

You're not treating each other well.
The truth is, when you first meet someone and fall in love with them, you treat them better

than anyone else. But when times get tough you treat them worse than anyone else, because the more emotionally involved you are, the more exaggerated your emotions become. It's bound to happen, but neither of you deserve to be badly treated especially by someone you love. If you no longer respect each other enough to make an effort, then you've got to call it quits. Love is based on respect.

Ask yourself 'is it normal that I am…'
Doing things that I would never dream of normally doing? Such as trying to memorise his password over his shoulder? Or drunk texting other guys on a night out?

Or in my case, I found myself crawling on my hands and knees in the middle of the night so I could check H's phone. He was a deep sleeper, so I'd wait until he was twitching and then I'd cough, to double-check he was fast asleep. If he didn't react, I'd roll out of bed, quietly landing on the floor. I'd crawl around the back of the bed on my hands and knees, reach my arm up and slide his phone off the bedside table. I'd then crawl back to my side of the bed so that in the worse case scenario, I could just dive under the duvet. Then I would turn the screen brightness down, before scrolling through his texts and dialled numbers. Every time I heard a noise my heart would stop. I should have realised at this point that something was seriously wrong. I was crawling around in the dark. Alone. In the middle of the night.

If you can't trust him.
You can't be with him. If you can't fully trust him, then you will end up constantly battling your fears about him. Sometimes you will let him know, but most of the time you will internalise your worry. Don't get crazy, just get real. If you really can't trust him, you probably have a good reason not to. Don't be with him.

Physically things aren't working.
Yes, bad or no sex can mean that something is wrong with your relationship. But both of these can be fixed by being open with each other. If you are going through a 'dry patch' and have lost your sex drive, the best thing to do is to talk about it. Yes, it's kind of embarrassing and, yes, it's easier to not talk about it, but the more you ignore a sex problem the more it will become an issue in your relationship. I know it's an awkward subject, but it's better to laugh and cringe your way through talking about it, than letting it ruin your relationship. If the sex isn't doing it for you, it doesn't mean he isn't, you need to be honest and open about what you like. Tell him what turns you on. The next time will be better.

You constantly feel jealous.
Jealousy can easily consume and kill your relationship. I always try to think about it from my boyfriend's point of view: what would I do and how would I feel if I was being constantly questioned? It's the one thing you need to work on by yourself, as no one else can cure your jealousy issues. But do speak to your friends and family about it. Remember that jealousy is your issue and it's not necessarily founded in truth.

You're arguing a lot.
This isn't necessarily a massive issue, as arguing can be healthy. I like to call them discussions. It can be totally constructive, as you should challenge each other and you need to stand up for what you believe in. I argued a lot with S. We would fight our corners but we would never fall out. However, if you are constantly arguing till your blood boils or saying unforgivable things – ready to hurl your phone across the room or threatening to call the police – that's not ok.

Are you still in love?
I think there is a major difference between being 'in love' with someone and loving them. Often when you have been with someone for a while, that initial crazy, all-consuming love is replaced by a deeper, more permanent kind of love, which is completely natural. But if you are no longer

in love, then although you may still love him, you have fallen out of love. There is no way of repairing this, it's simply how you feel. It's not his fault or your fault. It's just become a friendship more than a relationship.

You want different things.
When you first meet someone you want the same things. But lives change and you may begin to want different things. People don't stay the same and you may not be the same people who fell in love. It's very hard, but you need to both face up to this. Your relationship should always be based on the present not the past.

Unchangeable issues.
If he's violent, drinks, gambles or does drugs, you can not be with him. You can't change abusive behaviour and you can't stay in a destructive relationship with an addict. Only he can change and he won't do it if you stick around. Walk.

★ The 5 Rules ★

1. Are you happy?
2. Do you trust him completely?
3. Are you sexually compatible?
4. Do you respect each other?
5. Do you still want the same things?

9

IS HE CHEATING?

D ON'T GET ME WRONG, not all guys cheat and girls can cheat too. But it's something I've experienced in several of my relationships and I wish I'd had an older sister to sit me down and tell me, what I am about to tell you.

> UNDER NO CIRCUMSTANCES, DO YOU EVER TAKE BACK A CHEAT. IF HE'S DONE IT ONCE, HE'LL DO IT AGAIN.

Listen, if you forgive him, he'll lose respect for you and think he can get away with it, and if you stay with a cheating boyfriend, it will make you feel insecure and overly suspicious. You'll never fully trust him again. Believe me, I have been there. I forgave an ex-boyfriend for cheating, so many times, because I loved him and naively thought that was enough. What I should have done was break up with him, and never considered taking him back. It would have saved me a lot of heartbreak further down the line.

The S mistake.
Everyone questions why I fell in love with S, knowing his cheating track record. What can I say, the guy is the ultimate player and I made the mistake of thinking I could change him (one of the greatest dating game errors, people). S was highly manipulative and had a way of convincing

everyone he was sincere and, yes, I totally fell for it. When I first met S, I kept on thinking, how has he got such a reputation with girls? But as I got to know him – I warmed to his charm and after a while it became attractive.

S made me believe that he would change his ways for me and would never cheat on me, because I was his match, who would stand up to him and put him in his place. He repeatedly told me I was the complete opposite to L, his ex-girlfriend, who let him cheat on her. S completely convinced me. So I then convinced myself that I was the one in control and that I would be the one to change him.

Ironically, in the two months we were together, he acted like the best boyfriend I have ever had. He showed every sign of being seriously committed, he was wholeheartedly involved in my life and he met my friends and my family. He even went to meet my dad on his own so that he could get to know him properly, as he wanted to be part of my family. He came to my family home and played with my little brothers, he introduced me to his parents, he invited me on holiday, he gave me a key to his flat, he told me he loved me and he even said one day he could see himself marrying me. We spent every day together for two months. It was overwhelmingly reassuring and, yes, in hindsight, waaay too quick.

I finally found out that S had cheated on me thanks to Twitter and Facebook. He went to a party in Greece with his friend H. All night long, I got Twitter messages from girls telling me they had just seen him cheating on me. I ended up speaking to the friend of the girl who claimed she had slept with S. It quickly became sickeningly clear that S had cheated on me, the details were all too specific to have been made up. I felt like I had been punched. I really couldn't believe that after everything he had said, that he had cheated on me.

He called me the next day. I ignored his call as I wanted to talk face-to-face when he got back. But after receiving even more messages from girls, I knew I had to confront him. He picked up and denied everything. I tried getting angry, I tried getting upset, I tried calling his bluff, I tried everything. It was only when I made him feel guilty that he finally admitted to cheating. I burst into tears and told him that I didn't know what to do with myself because it had happened to me so many times and that I didn't deserve so much pain. That's when he eventually caved in and admitted what he had done.

I later found out that S had cheated on me with at least seven girls, even while I was sleeping alone in his bed while he was out partying in London. Lesson well and truly learnt: follow the dating game rules and never go out with anyone who has a history of cheating. I will never make that mistake ever again.

If your boyfriend has cheated on you.
It's really important that you know it's not your fault, you have done absolutely nothing wrong. Don't blame yourself. It's his problem and his issue with commitment, he'll do it again. Just think 'lucky escape' and pity him.

Don't put up and shut up.
Seriously, why should you put up with someone cheating on you when you can and will find someone who will love and respect you? Have some self-worth, know that you can do better and believe that you will find someone who will treat you with the respect you deserve.

★ Spotting the Signs ★

1. Always trust your female intuition. Sometimes you just know when something doesn't quite add up.
2. He keeps his phone face down on silent. One of my exes used to keep his phone on airplane mode, so he couldn't receive calls or texts. He claimed it was because he didn't want anyone to bother him.
3. Find out his dating past. As much as you want to be the girl that changes him, if he's cheated on his exes, he will cheat on you.
4. He's obsessively clean – always showering when he comes back from a night out.
5. When you can see he is online on Whatsapp, but doesn't pick up his phone or reply to you.
6. He calls you generic nicknames because he doesn't want to get your name mixed up with someone elses.
7. He can't get his story straight.
8. If he can't look you in the eye when you ask him where he has been.

10

BREAK UP & MOVE ON

THIS IS THE HARDEST PART of the dating game, but everyone goes through it and eventually everyone gets over it. Remember that you've never wasted your time, as being in love is one of the greatest feelings out there. But for now you need to stop having any contact with him. You need to stop speaking, texting, emailing and seeing him, as you now need closure. Accept it is over. Don't waste your time on the what ifs?, should I's?, why me's? and the but he's? And focus on yourself. It's totally true: sometimes the greatest power, is the power of goodbye.

When I break up with someone I do this thing called 'The Ceremony', where I go to my mum's house carrying all the tokens my ex-boyfriend has given me. Mementos like letters and photos which an ex has left at mine. We go into the garden and put it all into a big metal drum, douse it with oil and then set it alight and then we play some girl power anthem. I've had quite a few ceremonies! Trust me, it's really therapeutic and liberating. And definitely begins the separation process.

The next step is to be patient, because it can take weeks to start feeling better – don't feel like you have to rush through it and get over the break-up as quickly as possible. For the first

week, just cry, let your emotions out. Hang out with your mum and your friends, let them cook for you and watch films. If you have a job, see it as a godsend, because it will keep you distracted and busy. In those first few painful weeks you think it will never get better, but trust me, it does. In time you will feel much better. I promise.

The break-up stages:
1. Feeling rejected and alone
2. Anger and upset
3. Was it a waste of my time?
4. Will we get back together?
5. Acceptance

THE BREAK-UP SURVIVAL GUIDE

Stage one (first few weeks)
1. Cut off all contact. You need space and this only comes from deleting him from your life.

2. Delete him from your Facebook, Twitter and Instagram. You don't need to know what he is up to and you need to stop obsessing about what he is doing or how he is coping. Right now you need to focus entirely on yourself.

3. Tell your mutual friends you don't want to hear what he is up to. It's just way too much this early on and you both need to respect each other's privacy.

4. Don't spread rumours about him or speak openly badly about him. Bitterness is not attractive. Don't waste your energy.

5. 'The Ceremony'.

6. Remove him from your world. Pretend he is stranded on a desert island. It sounds dramatic, but it helps. You need to know that you can't contact him. He's not there any more.

7. Make a list of all the reasons why you broke up. Nostalgia is dangerous, as you forget the bad times and only remember the good. Store a list on your phone, for those moments of weakness, so you can read them and remember why this is happening.

8. Don't hold back the tears, because they will come out eventually and you need to process your emotions. If you get upset, just cry your eyes out. I always find myself crying in the car for some reason. I'll have one of those situations where I pull up to the traffic lights in tears and then I turn to see someone looking at me. Awkward.

9. See your friends. Go out for dinner, or to the cinema. Don't go out partying yet. If you go out too soon, you will compare everyone to your ex.

10. Don't have a one-night stand. It will leave you feeling much worse then you did before.

11. Spend quality time with your friends. When S and I broke up I went on holiday with my friend. We lay on the beach all day, every day. We didn't do much in the evenings just eat and sleep. I was so drained of emotions that I didn't have much energy to do anything, I cried a lot too. But three days in I properly laughed. My friend couldn't get over it, she kept on saying 'Oh my god, you've actually laughed'. There is always a breakthrough. When you start laughing, you start mending.

Stage two (a month in)

1. Go out and have fun. You'll know when you are ready. Don't push yourself, you don't want to worry about going out and getting publicly upset, so don't drink too much. Emotional drunkness will not make you feel better.

2. Stop talking about him. It's boring for your friends and it's not doing you any good reliving it over and over again. Drop him.

3. Get your hair done. I had highlights after I broke up with S, which was really liberating. If you look better, you will feel better. New chapter, new haircut, new you.

4. Don't get with guys. It's still too soon and you need to be in a man-free zone. Just have fun with your friends.

5. Don't agonise about what he is doing. It's not a race, you need to focus on yourself right now. Quit obsessing.

Stage three (a few months later)

1. Don't rush into another relationship. Starting a whole new relationship on top of trying to get over someone else requires way too much multi-tasking and it will only temporarily distract you from your break-up. You need to focus on yourself. Don't be with someone just because you don't want to be single and don't use men to distract you! Remember all the good things about not being tied down. Read Chapter One.

2. Don't meet up with him yet. It's too soon and seeing him in person will trigger any unresolved emotions you may still have. I would wait until you feel much stronger before you have any contact with him. Even now S will text me if he hears things about me, exes can't help it, but you can help yourself by waiting till you feel ready to reply.

3. Break up with his family. You can't get over someone if you carry on hanging out with his

family, because they will be a constant reminder of your ex. When I broke up with H, I was still so close to his mum. The problem was, we still spoke a lot about H, which stopped me getting over him. It became an emotional rollercoaster that I couldn't deal with, so I also had to break up with her. We met in a café in Guildford and both cried. It was necessary but seriously hard.

NEVER GET BACK WITH AN EX

You plus him doesn't equal a relationship.
Look, let's be honest, we have all been tempted to get back with an ex and when that text arrives in your inbox from them, yes, it brings back a hell of a lot of suppressed feelings. He wants to meet up, be friends, go for a drink, asks for you back, tells you he misses you. Whatever he says you have got to remember one simple thing: it didn't work out for a reason.

You plus him doesn't equal a happy relationship.
Yes, you miss him, but it's the guy you first fell in love with who you want back, not the guy you broke up with. Yes, it is a head-fuck, but ultimately it just didn't work out and the second time will only be worse! Trust me...

Too much damage has been done.
The trust is broken. It can only temporarily be mended before cracks begin to show.

I got it wrong.. I fucked up badly.. I took what we had for granted... It's the worst mistake of my life... We can work - I know we can... This has taught me so much.. I needed this to change

Nothing you will ever say will make me want to get back together with you.

That's a real shame... People make mistakes.. We could be incredible together.. I know that you know that... You said it yourself that part of you still loves me and all of me loves you back... I am yours.

It's just too soon.
It's the wrong thing to do, because nothing will
have changed. It's the comfort you are going back
to, not the damaged relationship. If you've been
apart for years as friends and you still think
about him and wonder 'what if?', then you may
be the exception to the rule and it may be worth
giving it another shot. But in the short-term; it's
just far too soon.

Once a cheat, always a cheat.
I made a mistake by going out with S as he had
history of cheating. But I put it right by not
giving him a second chance. No one knows how
hard he tried to get me back (see texts on p139
and opposite). For weeks he kept telling me how
much he loved me. I told him there was nothing
he could do, that I didn't tolerate cheating and
that was the end of it. I think he turned his
pain into anger by having a very public rebound
relationship and telling everyone he hated me
and didn't care about me. But, whatever. I knew
I was right. I had learnt from my mistakes and I
knew the dating game.

Do you think we can be together again in the future?... I know i'll have to work for it but i will.. What we had was different to anything I've ever felt...

You really are special to me..

I don't really think I could ever trust you again... You ruined it. And I don't think a conscience is something you can develop ... You don't seem to have any sign of one.

You were special to me but now I realise I just didn't really know you that well.

★ The 5 Rules ★

1. Erase him from your life
2. Let out your emotions
3. Focus on yourself
4. Don't rebound into another relationship
5. Never get back with an ex

START AGAIN

Turn back to Chapter One. Remember that heartbreak looks a lot better in time and that when a relationship doesn't work out it's just a test run. You are getting to know what you actually want and need all the time. Every break-up and breakdown will make you that much stronger and that much more sure of what you want in your next relationship.

Be lucky.

ACKNOWLEDGEMENTS

I think first and foremost I need to thank my parents, Clive and Fiona, they have brought me up to have a very clear understanding of what is right and wrong. They each have their different ways of doing it, but they have supported me through the highs and lows of every one of my relationships. I'm sure some of my horrendous decisions have tested their unconditional love for me, but they have always passed with flying colours.

I am grateful for my friends and their constant support. No matter how annoying I was or how little they respected my decisions, they always stood by me through thick and thin and accepted my constant need to learn from my many mistakes.

To the people who helped this book become reality. Flora and Emily at Emerge, Ruth and Clare and of course the Quadrille team, specifically Romilly. I think we have created something we are all proud of and hope that it will go towards helping and empowering women to be strong, make the right decisions and ultimately be happy.

And finally, without my ex-boyfriends there probably wouldn't be this book. So, in the least cringeworthy way, I would like to thank them, for 'making me that much stronger'.

Editorial director: Anne Furniss
Creative director: Helen Lewis
Editor: Romilly Morgan
Project design: Two Associates
Design assistant: Emily Lapworth, Gemma Hogan
Production: Sasha Hawkes, Vincent Smith

First published in 2014 by
Quadrille Publishing Limited
www.quadrille.co.uk

ISBN 987 184949 504 2
Printed in China

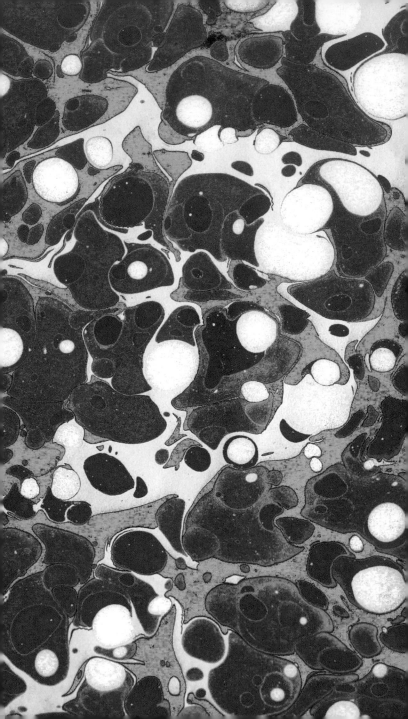